READY, SET, DRAW!

CREEPY CRAWLIES

AILIN CHAMBERS

 Gareth Stevens
PUBLISHING

Please visit our website, **www.garethstevens.com**. For a free color catalog of all our high-quality books, call toll free 1-800-542-2595 or fax 1-877-542-2596.

Library of Congress Cataloging-in-Publication Data

Chambers, Ailin.
Creepy Crawlies / by Ailin Chambers.
p. cm. — (Ready, set, draw!)
Includes index.
ISBN 978-1-4824-0912-3 (pbk.)
ISBN 978-1-4824-0913-0 (6-pack)
ISBN 978-1-4824-0911-6 (library binding)
1. Insects in art — Juvenile literature. 2. Invertebrates in art — Juvenile literature.. 3. Drawing — Technique — Juvenile literature. I. Chambers, Ailin. II. Title.
NC783.C43 2015
743.6—d23

First Edition

Published in 2015 by
Gareth Stevens Publishing
111 East 14th Street, Suite 349
New York, NY 10003

Copyright © Arcturus Holdings Limited

Editors: Samantha Hilton, Kate Overy and Joe Harris
Illustrations: Dynamo Limited
Design concept: Keith Williams
Design: Dynamo Limited and Notion Design
Cover design: Ian Winton

Printed in the United States of America

CPSIA compliance information: Batch #CS15GS: For further information contact Gareth Stevens, New York, New York at 1-800-542-2595.

CONTENTS

8

RHINOCEROS
BEETLE

10

SCORPION

12

PRAYING
MANTIS

14

RED ANT

16

BUTTERFLY

18

TARANTULA

20

COCKROACH

22

HORNET

24

CENTIPEDE

26

HUMMINGBIRD
HAWK-MOTH

29

LOCUST

GRAB THESE!

Are you ready to create some amazing pictures? Wait a minute! Before you begin drawing, you will need a few important pieces of equipment.

PENCILS

You can use a variety of drawing tools, such as pens, chalks, pencils, and paints. But to begin, use an ordinary pencil.

PAPER

Use a clean sheet of paper for your final drawings. Scrap paper is useful and cheap for your practice work.

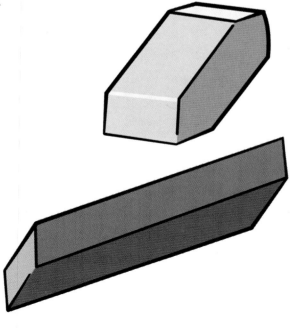

ERASERS

Everyone makes mistakes! That's why every artist has a good eraser. When you erase a mistake, do it gently. Erasing too hard will ruin your drawing and possibly even rip it.

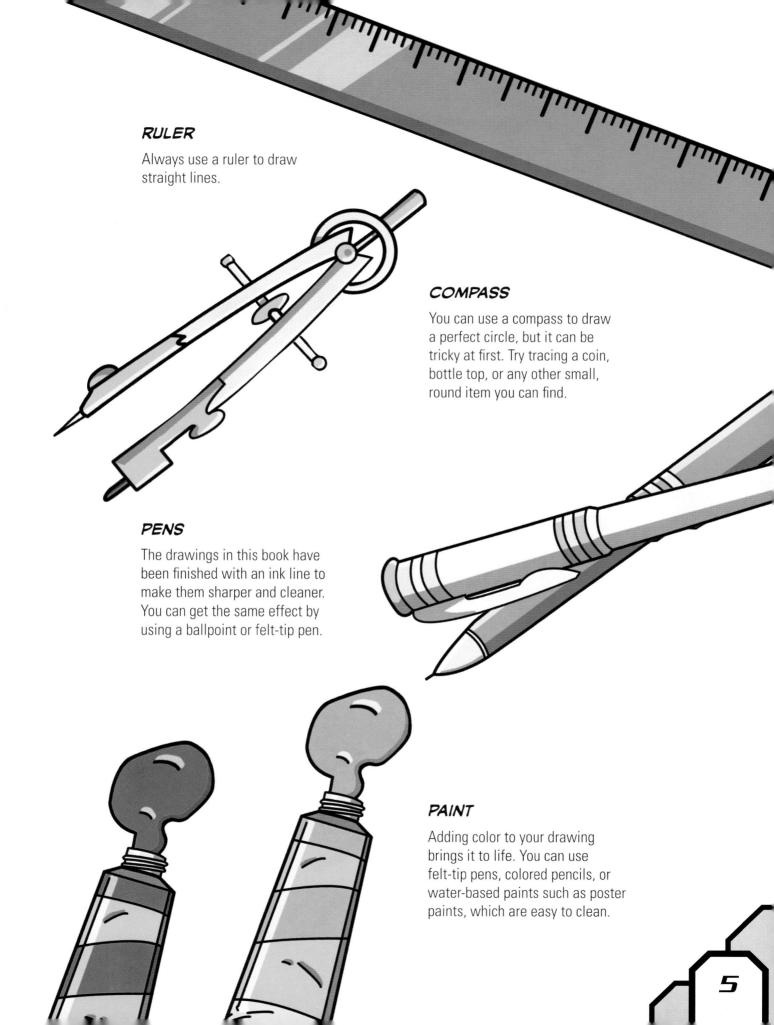

RULER

Always use a ruler to draw straight lines.

COMPASS

You can use a compass to draw a perfect circle, but it can be tricky at first. Try tracing a coin, bottle top, or any other small, round item you can find.

PENS

The drawings in this book have been finished with an ink line to make them sharper and cleaner. You can get the same effect by using a ballpoint or felt-tip pen.

PAINT

Adding color to your drawing brings it to life. You can use felt-tip pens, colored pencils, or water-based paints such as poster paints, which are easy to clean.

GETTING STARTED

In this book, we use a simple two-color system to show you how to draw a picture. Just remember: New lines are blue lines!

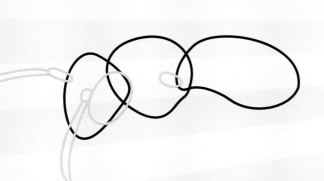

STARTING WITH STEP 1

The first lines you will draw are very simple shapes. They will be shown in blue. You should draw them with a normal pencil.

ADDING MORE DETAIL

As you move on to the next step, the lines you have already drawn will be shown in black. The new lines for that step will appear in blue.

FINISHING YOUR PICTURE

When you reach the final stage you will see the image in full color with a black ink line. Inking a picture means tracing the main lines with a black pen. After the ink dries, use your eraser to remove all the pencil lines before adding your color.

ADDING MOVEMENT

Here are some fun ways to make your bugs look as though they're really moving. Follow these tips, and pretty soon they'll be crawling or buzzing off your page!

FLOATING

Show how a butterfly flutters through the air by adding a small, dotted line that traces the path it has flown.

SPEED LINES

Bugs such as cockroaches move quickly, but this can be difficult to show on paper. Add simple lines coming away from the the bug's back end. Draw a puff of smoke and it will really look as if it's zooming along.

VIBRATION LINES

You can easily make the wings of your bug look as though they are moving back and forth. Just add simple vibration lines that follow the line of the edges of the wings.

SNAP, SNAP!

A sudden movement, such as a fierce snap from a claw, can be shown by adding a cartoon flash. This spiky shape will give your drawing some extra drama. Look out!

RHINOCEROS BEETLE

The rhinoceros beetle is a large insect with two huge horns on its head, which it uses for fighting and digging. It also has very thick and shiny "armor."

STEP 1

First, draw the horns. Follow the shape on the right, then add a long oval for the beetle's body.

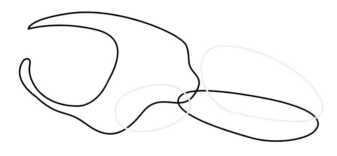

STEP 2

Next, add two ovals to create the beetle's face and the covering for its wing.

STEP 3

Draw some details on the horns, and add three ovals to begin making the beetle's legs.

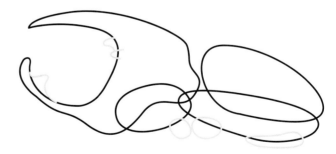

STEP 4

Add the legs and the spike on the beetle's body. Then, add a curved line across the horns.

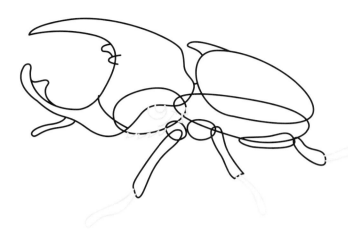

STEP 5

Finally, add the last part of the legs, and complete the outline of the head as shown. Then, add its eye.

STEP 6

A rhinoceros beetle may look fierce, but it's actually harmless. To make its body look shiny, add a white line across its back.

SCORPION

A scorpion is part of the spider family. It has eight legs and a huge pair of claws. Its long, thin tail curves over its back, and there is a nasty stinger at the end of it!

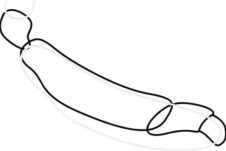

STEP 1

Begin to draw the scorpion's body by linking together these four shapes.

STEP 2

Draw over the first outline with these three shapes. The two small ovals mark the start of its tail.

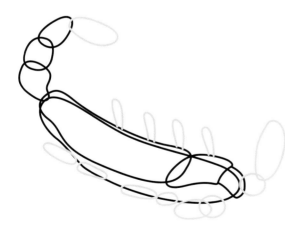

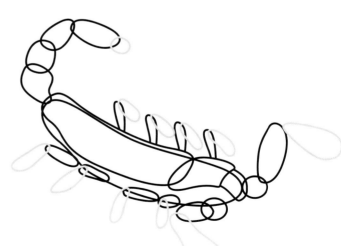

STEP 3

These small loops are the start of the legs. There are four on each side and two for each of the claws at the front. Add another oval to the tail.

STEP 4

Add some more loops to form the next segments of the legs, claws, and tail. A segment is part of an insect's body.

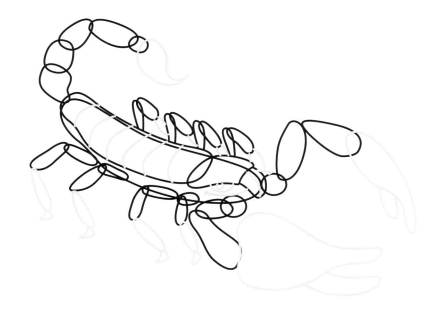

STEP 5

Draw the last segments of the legs, and add six stripes across the main body. Then, add the large claws and the sharp stinger on the tail. Finally, draw the scorpion's face.

STEP 6

Color your scorpion red. It may have a smiling face, but don't be fooled. The sneaky look in its eye suggests that it may be about to strike!

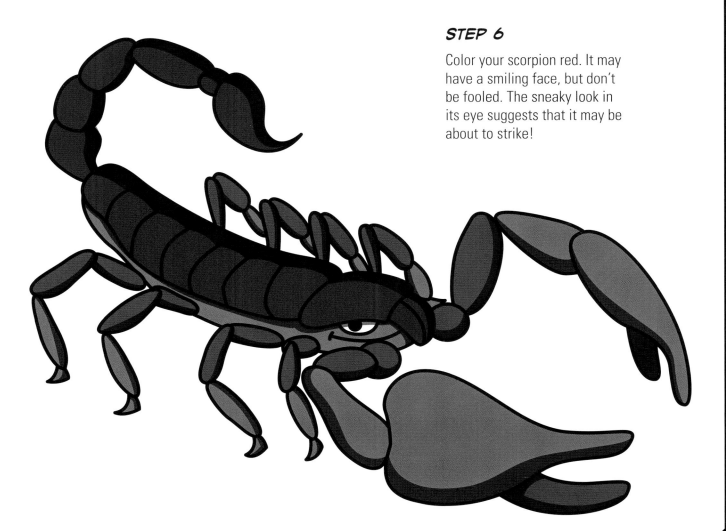

PRAYING MANTIS

A praying mantis is a strange insect. It has a triangular head, a long body, and large front legs. The front legs are folded in a way that makes the bug look like it's praying.

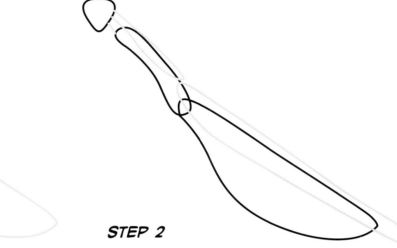

STEP 1

Draw the insect's three main body parts: its small, triangular head and two longer shapes.

STEP 2

Link the head to the main body, and add two narrow shapes to form its wings.

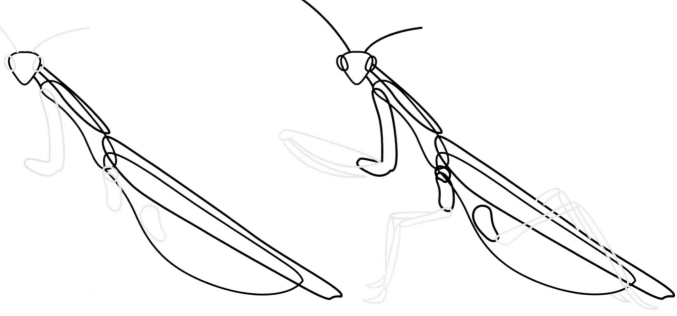

STEP 3

Now, add its eyes and long antennae. Three small shapes begin the middle and back legs, and a shape like the letter J is the start of its front legs.

STEP 4

Next, add the insect's long, thin back legs and its bent middle legs. Finish the large front legs.

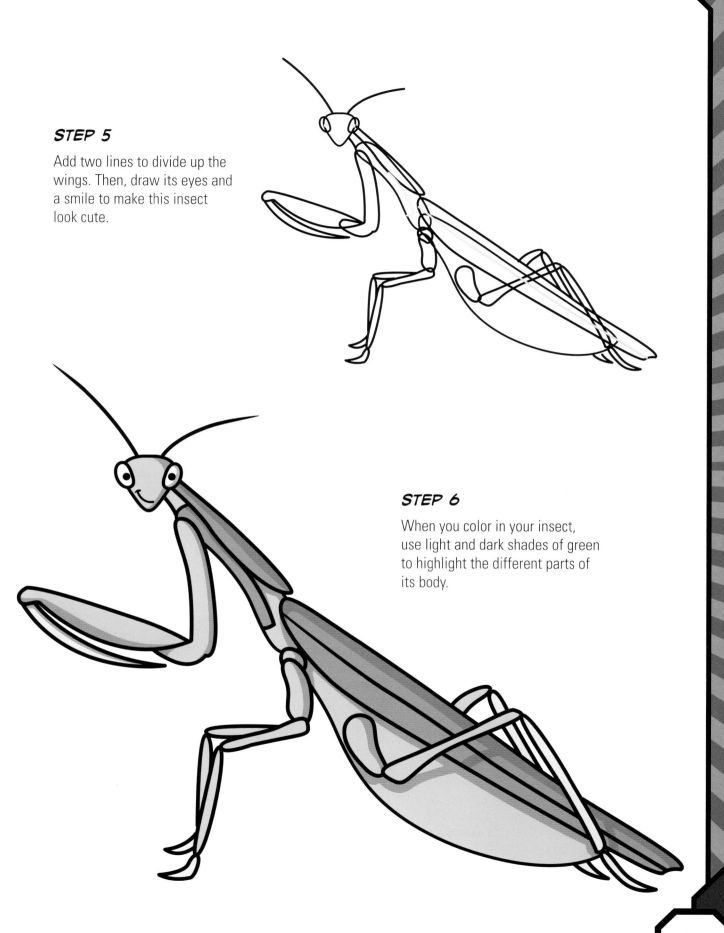

STEP 5

Add two lines to divide up the wings. Then, draw its eyes and a smile to make this insect look cute.

STEP 6

When you color in your insect, use light and dark shades of green to highlight the different parts of its body.

RED ANT

Red ants are sometimes known as fire ants because of their reddish color. These tiny but fierce insects live in large groups called colonies.

STEP 1

First, draw the ant's body with these bean-like shapes. Make sure the head is slightly flattened.

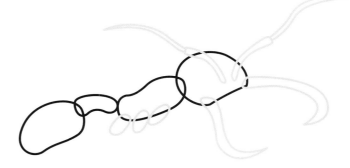

STEP 2

Next, add two sharp pincers and long antennae. Draw three ovals for the start of the leg joints.

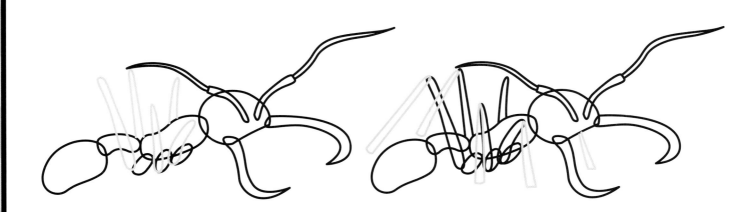

STEP 3

Add long segments to the ant's skinny legs.

STEP 4

Add another set of segments to the legs, so they point downwards.

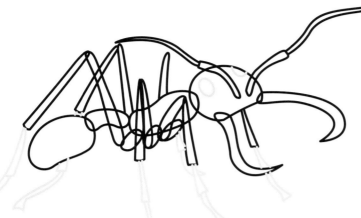

STEP 5

Draw the final segments of the ant's six legs, and add a pair of eyes.

STEP 6

Red ants spend most of their time on the forest floor. Color them with red and brown color to keep them hidden!

BUTTERFLY

Butterflies come in many different colors and patterns. This one is yellow and orange, but you could choose any colors you like.

STEP 1

First, draw a small, round head, a sausage shape for the body and two antennae.

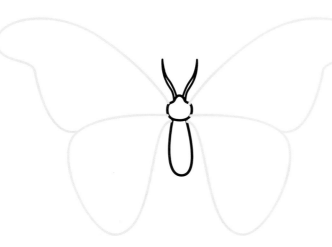

STEP 2

Now, draw the butterfly's large and beautiful wings. Try to make the two wings exactly the same shape.

STEP 3

Add some markings to the wings. Then, draw some stripes on the insect's body.

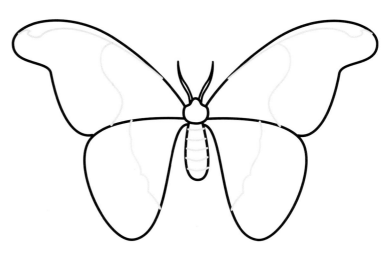

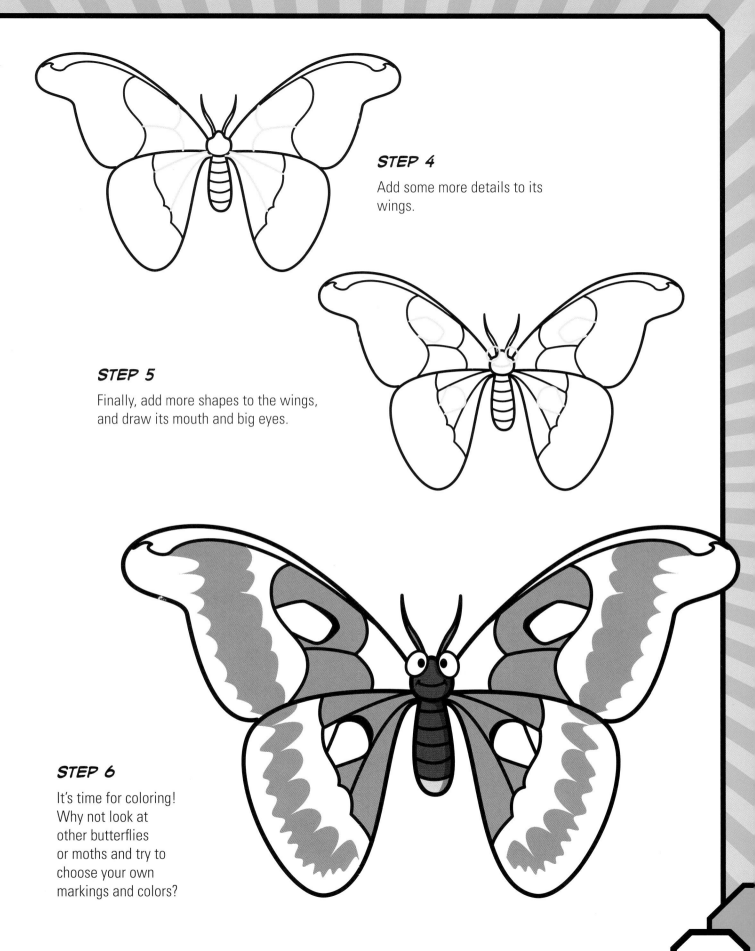

STEP 4

Add some more details to its wings.

STEP 5

Finally, add more shapes to the wings, and draw its mouth and big eyes.

STEP 6

It's time for coloring! Why not look at other butterflies or moths and try to choose your own markings and colors?

TARANTULA

A tarantula is spider with a large, hairy body. It has eight stripy legs, which are covered in tiny hairs. It hunts for food at night, catching insects and even small reptiles!

STEP 1

First, draw two overlapping ovals to make the body and head. Add a smaller shape to make the mouth.

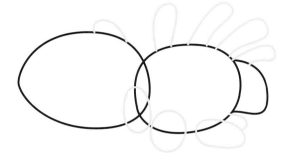

STEP 2

Next, draw four ovals and five sausage shapes to begin to form the spider's eight legs and one of its antennae.

STEP 3

Now, add some more segments to the spider's long, thin legs and its antenna.

STEP 4

Next, add more oval-shaped leg segments and the outline of the other antenna.

STEP 5

Complete the legs, then add curved zigzags along the outline of its head and body to make it look furry. Add large eyes and a line down the spider's mouth.

SUPER TIP!

Tarantulas are covered in tiny hairs that give them a slightly furry appearance.

- Draw the main body shape and color it in.

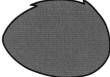

- Then, add short lines. Only use a few to make it look slightly furry.

STEP 6

We've colored our spider using black and orange. Each segment of the legs is a different color, to make a striped pattern.

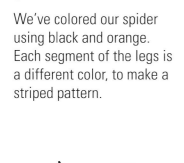

COCKROACH

A cockroach is a tough insect that has been around since the time of the dinosaurs! This six-legged bug can move very quickly. It likes to hide in dark corners.

STEP 1

First, draw these three shapes to make the insect's body and head.

STEP 2

Next, add some very long antennae to the cockroach's head.

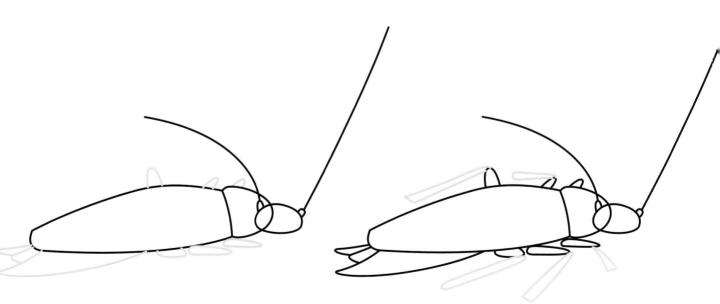

STEP 3

Draw three shapes at the back to make the folded wings, and add six ovals to start the legs.

STEP 4

Now, add five longer shapes to five of the ovals to give the insect proper legs.

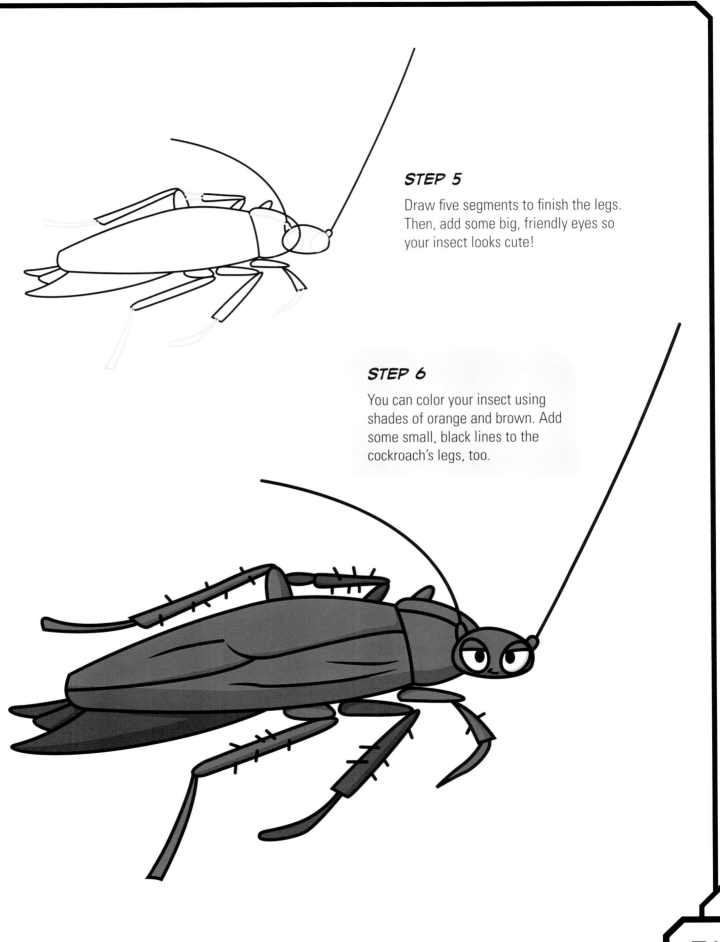

STEP 5

Draw five segments to finish the legs. Then, add some big, friendly eyes so your insect looks cute!

STEP 6

You can color your insect using shades of orange and brown. Add some small, black lines to the cockroach's legs, too.

HORNET

A hornet looks a bit like a wasp, only bigger. It has a smooth body, long wings, and black and yellow markings. But beware, this insect can give you a nasty sting!

STEP 1

First, draw three oval shapes to make the hornet's head and body.

STEP 2

Next, add the long antennae and one eye. Draw a small circle on the middle part of the hornet. This is where the wing joins on to the body.

STEP 3

Next, draw the long and thin wings. Add three ovals to begin drawing its legs.

STEP 4

Add more segments to create the hornet's long legs.

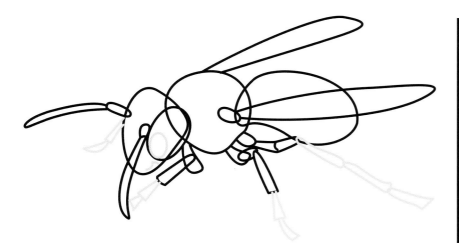

STEP 5

Finish the legs as shown above. Add a pupil to the insect's eye and a little, smiling mouth.

SUPER TIP!

- To create transparent wings for bugs, such as hornets, wasps, and bees, first draw vein lines.

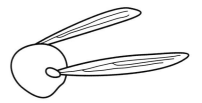

- Color the wings in a very light shade. Pale blue works best.

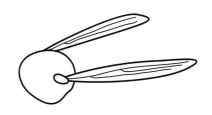

STEP 6

Yellow and black warn you to keep your distance from this super-sized stinger!

CENTIPEDE

The name centipede may mean "100 legs," but this bug actually has around 40. Its long body is made up of lots of segments. Each segment has its own pair of legs.

STEP 1

First, draw a long, curved line. You can make it any shape you want as long as you keep it slightly curved.

STEP 2

Starting at the back of your centipede, draw a very small egg shape. Move along the line, drawing the same shape again and again. Make each one slightly larger as you go.

STEP 3

Draw a small, curved line where each circle joins to start the legs.

STEP 4

Go over the legs again and make them look thicker.

STEP 5

Add the centipede's tail and antennae. Don't forget to draw big eyes, so your centipede can see where it's going.

STEP 6

Add a darker shade to the bottom edge of the circles when you're coloring. This will give the body a rounded shape.

SUPER TIP!

We've drawn our centipede in a straight line to show you how to do it, but you can pose yours any way you want to.

- Sketch your first line in any shape you want. Below, we've drawn a more curved line.

- Then, start building your circle shapes along the line.

HUMMINGBIRD HAWK-MOTH

This moth is sometimes mistaken for a bird! Its wings beat so fast that they make a humming sound as the moth hovers over flowers. Its long proboscis (the part that looks like a nose) dips into flowers and collects nectar.

STEP 1

First, draw a shape like this for the moth's body outline.

STEP 2

Add a large, flat wing to help your moth hover like a hummingbird. Add a pair of antennae and an oval for its leg.

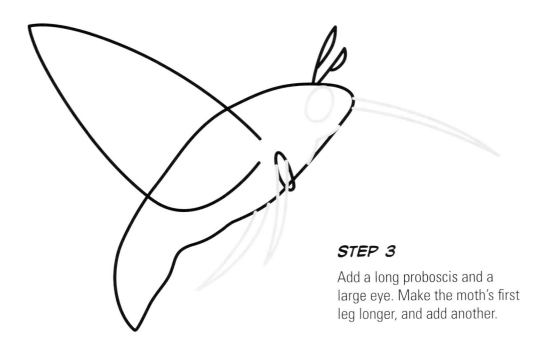

STEP 3

Add a long proboscis and a large eye. Make the moth's first leg longer, and add another.

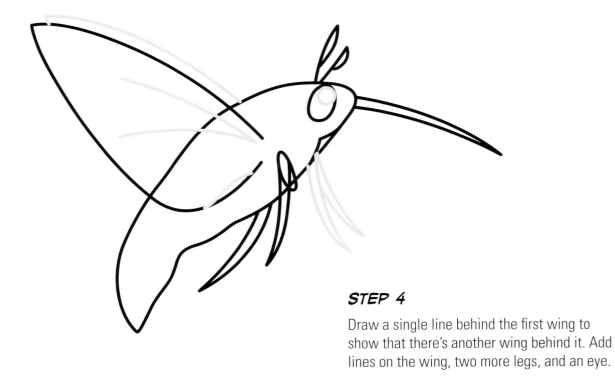

STEP 4

Draw a single line behind the first wing to show that there's another wing behind it. Add lines on the wing, two more legs, and an eye.

STEP 5

Draw more lines on the wing. Add curved lines across the back of its body.

STEP 6

Moths are not as colorful as butterflies. This one is mostly gray and brown.

A locust is an insect that belongs to the grasshopper family. It has long, powerful back legs that help it to leap through the air. It also has wings, so it can fly!

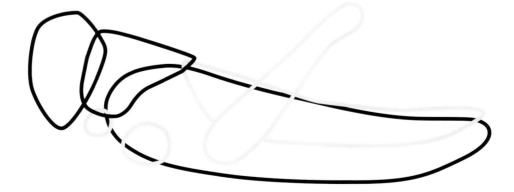

STEP 1

First, draw a long, curved body that leads up to a chunky neck. Add a teardrop-shaped head.

STEP 2

Next, add a wing case and the start of a long back leg. Then, draw two ovals. They will become the two front legs.

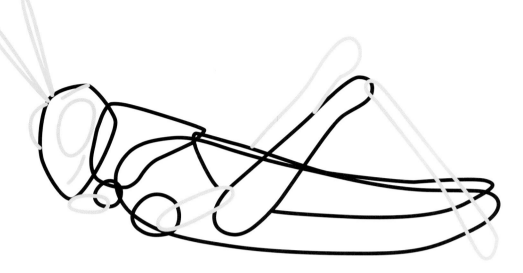

STEP 3

Draw a pair of short antennae. Add big eyes, an eyebrow, and a mouth. Draw more leg segments.

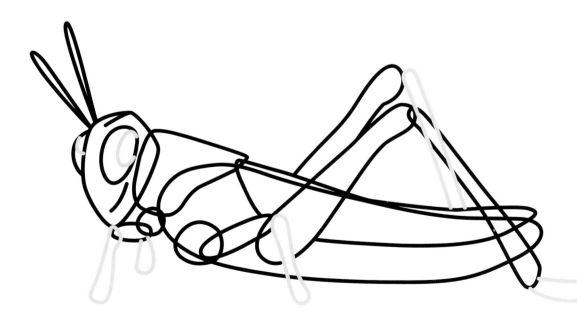

STEP 4

Finish the back legs, and add more segments to the other legs and detail to the eyes.

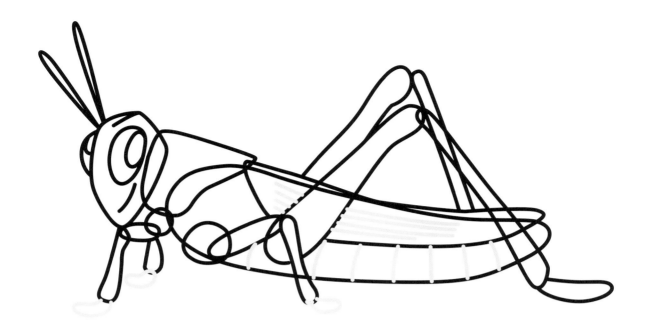

STEP 5

Draw the feet, and add some lines on the wing case and lower body.

STEP 6

Choose some different shades of yellow and orange for your locust. Now it's ready to hop off the page!

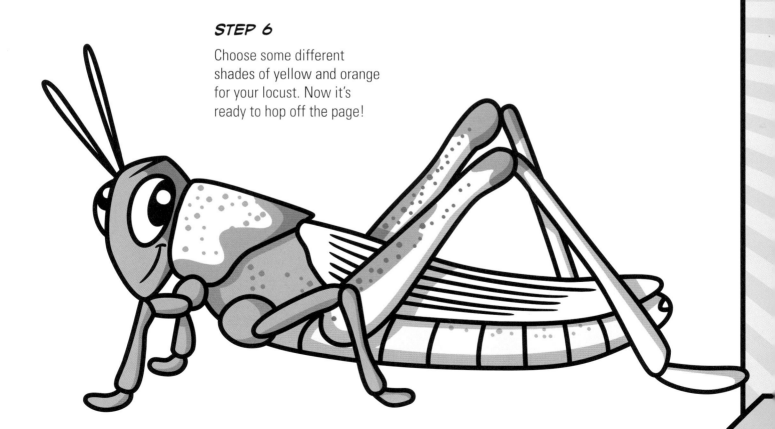

GLOSSARY

antennae Long, thin organs on the head of an insect that are used to touch and feel things.

colony A group of insects

nectar A sweet liquid produced by flowering plants.

pincer A claw.

proboscis A long, thin tube that forms part of the mouth of some insects.

pupil The dark center of the eye.

reptile An animal such as a snake or a lizard.

segment Part of an insect's body.

vein A thin line on the wing of an insect.

wing case A hard covering over the wings of an insect.

FURTHER READING

Insects: Step-By-Step Instructions for 26 Creepy Crawlies by Diana Fisher (Walter Foster Publishing, 2010)

What to Doodle? Creepy Crawlies! by Chuck Whelon (Dover Children's, 2011)

WEBSITES

animals.nationalgeographic.co.uk/animals/bugs/

www.dltk-kids.com/Crafts/insects/

www.dragoart.com/insects-c174-1.htm

INDEX